THE ASSOCIATION OF INCOME
AND
EDUCATIONAL ACHIEVEMENT
by Roy L. Lassiter, Jr.

UNIVERSITY OF FLORIDA PRESS / GAINESVILLE, FLORIDA, 1966

EDITORIAL COMMITTEE

Social Sciences Monographs

─────────────────────────────

PREFACE

In recent years, economists and others have given attention to education in terms of the economic rewards associated therewith. This study represents an attempt to broaden the scope of the investigations so as to relate the rewards explicitly to educational achievement for important segments of the population of the United States. Heretofore, most of the emphasis by others has been in terms of all males in the United States. Such analyses have been useful, but have necessarily obscured or ignored such factors as race, sex, region, and urban-rural location as these interact to influence the relationship between income and education.

This study employs correlation and regression methods in analyzing the association of income and education for important segments of the population. While these techniques have limitations, it is felt that they do provide an alternative and highly useful approach to investigating private incentives to make the educational investment. Furthermore, statistical tests of significance are employed to evaluate inter-group and intra-group differences. Such tests have been largely ignored in earlier investigations, in which all differences have been implicitly assumed to be statistically significant.

The author is indebted to the Inter-University Committee for Economic Research on the South for a grant to evaluate the significant dimensions of human capital in the South. This study is part of that investigation. In addition, credit is extended to the University of Florida Computing Center for computer time; to Miss LaHoma Riederer and Mr. Dale Moody of the College of Business Administration Computing Laboratory for programming and data processing assistance; and to Professors Ralph H. Blodgett and Milton Z. Kafoglis who reviewed the entire manuscript, and Professor Mary Jean Bowman who commented on one portion of the study.

Roy L. Lassiter, Jr.

Gainesville, Florida

CONTENTS

1. INTRODUCTION

This monograph purposes to explore the empirical relationship between income and years of school completed, and to utilize this relationship, as established, to examine differences in private economic incentives to invest in education among important segments of the population of the United States. Specifically, the relationship between income and education will be examined as it is affected by race, sex, age, urban-rural residence, and region to determine the differences among these groupings, and the impact which these differences have on private incentives to invest in education. While the major emphasis will be placed on the economics of educational decisions, there is no intent to minimize the influence of a host of non-economic factors. Furthermore, the concentration on formal education, as measured by years of school completed, should not be interpreted as an attempt to ignore the import of the extensive, more informal, but unfortunately less measurable, educational processes.

While it has long been obvious that there are costs and rewards associated with educational attainment, only in recent years have there been extensive attempts to evaluate the educational decision within the framework of investment theory. Such investigators as Houthakker, Miller, Schultz, *et al.* have explored the association of income and education and the implications of this association for investment in human capital.[1] The empirical evidence employed in these

1. See, for example, H. S. Houthakker, "Education and Income," *Review of Economics and Statistics*, February, 1959, pp. 24-28; Theodore W. Schultz, "Capital Formation by Education," *The Journal of Political Economy*, December, 1960, pp. 571-83; Herman P. Miller, "Annual and Lifetime Income in Relation to Education, 1939-1959," *The American Economic Review*, December, 1960, pp. 962-86; T. W. Schultz, *et al.*, "Investment in Human Beings," *The Journal of Political Economy*, Supplement, October, 1962, pp. 1-157; W. L. Hansen, "Total and Private Rates of Return to Investment in School-

studies has largely been that of the United States Bureau of the Census, supplemented with available education cost data. Typically, the analyses have employed estimates of arithmetic mean income associated with various levels of educational attainment to estimate the rewards to varying years of school completed. The costs have been expressed in terms of society's cost of providing education and the costs to the recipient of that education, including earnings foregone while attending school. The magnitude of the "returns" to the educational investment have alternatively been expressed as the additional lifetime income associated with increased education, the present value of this added income, and the rate of return over costs. With few exceptions, the studies to date have not dealt with the returns to education as influenced by such factors as race, sex, age, urban-rural residence, and region.[2] Furthermore, there have been no attempts to measure directly the degree of the association of income and education using correlation and regression techniques, to employ statistical tests of significance in evaluating the differences in returns to education, or to explore adequately recent evidence from the 1960 Census of Population.

DATA AND METHODOLOGY

The data employed in this study are from the 1950 and 1960 Censuses of Population and represent estimates of the

---

ing," *The Journal of Political Economy*, April, 1963, pp. 128-40. For a study which questions the utility of the "human capital" approach see John Vaizey, *The Economics of Education*, Glencoe, Ill., Free Press, 1962.

2. For two of the few investigations into the influence of some of these factors see Gary Becker, "Underinvestment in College Education," *The American Economic Review*, May, 1960, pp. 346-54; and Becker, *Human Capital*, New York, National Bureau of Economic Research, No. 80, 1964. Miller points out that, with the exception of Becker's work, differences in the association of income and education between whites and nonwhites have been either ignored or treated superficially. See Miller, "Income and Education: Does Education Pay Off?" in *Economics of Higher Education*, ed. Selma Mushkin, Washington, U.S. Department of Health, Education, and Welfare, OE50027, Bulletin, 1962, No. 5, p. 131.

total population characteristics as derived from sample census data. The data relating income and education in the 1950 Census volumes represent estimates derived from a 3 1/3 per cent sample of all census returns. The 1960 Census data were derived from either a 25 per cent sample of housing units and persons in group quarters, or a 20 per cent sub-sample of the original 25 per cent sample schedules.[3] In making the statistical tests of significance pertinent to this study, sample sizes were assumed to be the appropriate percentage of the total persons reported in the respective census tables.

Census data are not in a form directly suited to the purposes of this study or the techniques employed. The statistics relating income and education are presented in 72, 90, and 96 cell frequency tables with unequal and open-end class intervals for both variables. It was assumed that the midpoints of the class intervals were the means of the classes, and that the means of the open-end income classes were $20,000 for the 1950 Census data, and $16,000 and $25,000 for the two types of tabulations presented in the 1960 Census.[4] The open-end class of years of school completed was truncated at either 16 or 17 years, depending on the manner which the Census data were tabulated.[5]

Further difficulties in utilizing the Census information arise from the form in which the tabulations are reported.

3. For further discussion of the sampling procedures and the over-all estimates see the census volumes cited in this monograph.

4. This procedure essentially follows that of Miller and others at the Bureau of the Census in estimating mean incomes from Census data. See Miller, "Annual and Lifetime Income," p. 965. The mean of $16,000 for certain of the 1959 data was suggested by Mr. Henry S. Shryock, Jr., Acting Chief, Population Division, Bureau of the Census (letter to the author dated June 4, 1963). The mean of $25,000 for certain tabulations in the 1960 Census was considered appropriate in view of the data presented in the *Subject Report. Occupation by Earnings and Education. Final Report PC(2)-7B.*

5. Data on degrees awarded indicate that the mean educational achievement in the classes 16 years of school completed and over and 17 years of school completed and over would not be appreciably higher than 16 or 17 years. Thus the procedure used would not materially influence the overall regression and correlation results.

Data on whites and nonwhites are not reported separately in some cases, and those for the South are included in the totals for the United States. Separation of the data into categories suited to the purposes of the analysis was achieved by punching cards for the various total and subtotal categories and utilizing a computer subtraction process to obtain the requisite distributions.

Several functions were fitted to the data in an attempt to find the "best" fit.[6] The arithmetically linear form $Y = a + bX$ (where Y = income and X = years of school completed) almost uniformly gave the highest correlation coefficients, although the $\log Y = a + bX$ function yielded approximately similar results in some cases, and there were a few instances in which the indexes of correlation from quadratic functions were slightly greater than the linear coefficients. Most of the analyses in this study will employ the $Y = a + bX$ expressions of the relationship between income and education, with occasional references to the function which is linear in logarithms of income.

Problems of interpretation of Census data exist in terms of the income concept employed (total money income rather than earnings). Furthermore, the "year of school completed" variable is not homogeneous between census years, nor among the segments of the population in given years. For example, it is widely recognized that a "year of school completed" for nonwhites is not generally equivalent to that accomplished by whites, even though the calendar input is the same.[7] Unfortunately, statistical evidence regarding the equivalence of "years of school completed" among groups and regions is so

6. Specifically, the functions employed were $Y = a + bX$; $\log Y = a + bX$; $1/Y = a + bX$; $1/Y = a + bl/X$; and $Y = a + bX + cX^2$. It might be suspected that the actual relationship between income and education would "best" be described by some step function, for which the arithmetically linear form is the "best fitting" approximation among those tried.

7. For a discussion of this problem see Miller, "Income and Education," p. 132, and in the same volume the paper by T. W. Schultz, pp. 96, 97.

limited as to preclude a meaningful attempt to standardize the education variable.

Further qualification of the adequacy of the regression coefficients as a measure of the increase in income associated with additional school completed must be made in recognition of the influences of such factors as ability, determination, and family attitudes and resources. All of these tend to be positively related to income and are reflected in the estimates of the returns to education. Thus, the interpretation of the regression coefficients must take cognizance of the interaction of these factors with additional schooling. The data also have the weakness of giving the income of persons completing school at some earlier time, rather than that which will be received in the future by persons completing the same number of years of school now. In other words, the income estimates and/or rates of return derived from the cross-sectional census data do not reflect either the secular growth of the economy or the increasing quality of education received. To this extent, the estimates developed in this study understate the worth of education.

The preceding discussion has centered on the nature and limitations of Census data relating income and education. In spite of these limitations, these data constitute the best available for the purposes of an investigation such as this one. Of course, such limitations will be recognized in the inferences drawn and the conclusions reached.

Order of Presentation

Chapter 2 will present the empirical relationship between income and education in 1949 and 1959, as affected by race, sex, age, urban-rural residence, and region. Differences in private incentives to invest in education will be analyzed in Chapter 3, and the implications of the association of income and education will be discussed in Chapter 4.

2. THE EMPIRICAL RELATIONSHIP BETWEEN INCOME AND EDUCATION

Intuitively, the association of income and education would be expected to vary with race, sex, age, urban-rural residence, and region as these factors influence employment opportunities, participation in the labor force, and quality of education received. This investigation, as previously mentioned, will examine these attributes as they influence the relationship between income and education. However, primary emphasis will be given to the male component of the population because of the higher proportion of males participating in the labor force, and thus the relatively greater direct economic significance of education in this group. Furthermore, the bulk of the analysis will employ 1959 data because of their greater current relevance and the greater detail in which they were reported.

INCOME AND EDUCATION: PERSONS 25 YEARS OF AGE AND OLDER

There was a low positive, but statistically significant, correlation of income and education for the overall race and sex groupings of persons twenty-five years of age and older in both 1949 and 1959 (Table 1).[1] The degree of this association increased for all classes from 1949 to 1959, as did the mean incomes and regression coefficients. The mean income of white males was higher than those of the other classes in both years, and the absolute differences between mean in-

---

1. The correlation coefficients would be increased somewhat if Sheppard's correction were employed. This adjustment was not made because the uncorrected correlation coefficients are most appropriate when subject to statistical tests of significance. See R. A. Fisher, *Statistical Methods for Research Workers*, New York, Hafner, 1958, p. 186.

come of this class and those of the other groups increased from 1949 to 1959. In both years white females had the highest average educational achievement, and nonwhite males had

TABLE 1

MEASURES OF THE ASSOCIATION OF INCOME AND YEARS OF SCHOOL
COMPLETED FOR PERSONS 25 YEARS OF AGE AND OLDER IN
THE UNITED STATES, BY RACE AND SEX, 1949 AND 1959

Year, Race and Sex	Mean Income	Mean Years of School Completed	Correlation Coefficient	Regression Coefficient	Standard Error of Estimate
1949	$			$	$
White male	3,375	9.4	0.31[*,a]	276[*,b]	3,102
Nonwhite male	1,663	6.2	0.32[*,a]	112[*,b]	1,283
White female	1,585	10.0	0.23[*,a]	120[*,b]	1,816
Nonwhite female	889	7.0	0.33[*,a]	79[*,b]	902
1959					
White male	5,481	10.0	0.43[*,a]	461[*,b]	3,603
Nonwhite male	2,939	7.3	0.39[*,a]	211[*,b]	2,103
White female	2,224	10.1	0.32[*,a]	196[*,b]	2,069
Nonwhite female	1,486	7.9	0.40[*,a]	143[*,b]	1,319

*Significantly different from zero at the 0.01 level. Degrees of freedom determined as being 0.033N for 1949 and 0.25N for 1959, where N = the number of persons reported in the respective census table. Degrees of freedom associated with the various categories varied from 70,713 to 10,445,418.

a. All differences ≥ 0.02 (approximate) between coefficients are statistically significant at the 0.01 level.

b. Differences amounting to $5.00 (approximate) are statistically significant at the 0.01 level. Standard errors of all regression coefficients were estimated from those of "blown up" data by adjusting for sample size.

Source: Computed from data presented in the U.S. Census of Population, 1950, in Special Report P-E No. 5B and U.S. Census of Population, 1960, Final Report PC(1)-1D.

the lowest average of school years completed. In 1949 the correlation coefficients did not vary greatly between groups, except for the white female class where the correlation was substantially lower than for the other groups. In 1959 differences between all correlation coefficients were statistically significant, and again the lowest coefficient existed for the white female group.[2]

The regression coefficient was highest in both years for white males and lowest for nonwhite females. In 1959 the additional income for nonwhite males associated with an additional year of school completed was slightly higher than for white females. There was substantial absolute and relative variation about the regression lines for all classes, indicating that low percentages of the variations of income were "explained" by the regression.

There was a pronounced effect of age on the association of income and education for all of the overall race and sex classes in both 1949 and 1959. For both races and sexes, with the exception of nonwhite females, the lowest degree of association between income and education, and the lowest regression coefficients, existed in the 25-34 age group (Table 2). Mean incomes, correlation coefficients, and regression coefficients increased with age for all classes, at least through the 35-44 age category. The patterns exhibited by the race and sex groups varied somewhat, although there were similarities exhibited by the nonwhite classes. For example, the mean incomes and regression coefficients for nonwhites increased through the age 35-44 class and declined with age thereafter in both census years. In 1959 the mean income and regression coefficient for white males also declined after the 35 to 44 age class. Mean incomes and regression coefficients for white females increased at least through the 45 to 54 age class in both years, and in 1959 both the correlation and regression coefficients for white females increased with age throughout the specified age classes.

2. The degree of association between income and education for white females would be expected to be lower than for the other classes because a lower proportion are in the labor force and thus generating earnings.

The foregoing analysis has demonstrated that the association of income and education for persons in the 25 years of age and older classes can be altered by significant shifts in the age distribution of the population. The age distribution of the United States population shifted between 1949 and 1959 with pronounced decreases in the percentage of persons in the 25 to 34 age groups, slight reductions in the percentage of the persons in the 35 to 44 age groups, and an increase in the percentage of persons in the older age groups for all race and sex classes (Table 3). The correlation between income and education for all white males as a group would tend to be increased by the shift in the age distribution which occurred in this class. On the other hand, the changes in the association of income and education for nonwhite males would be influenced to a lesser extent because income appears to be less variable with age for this group. The relatively older nonwhite female population in 1959 would tend to be characterized by a lower degree of association between income and education than that which would have existed had the age distribution of this class been unchanged. The striking reduction in the percentage of white females in the child-bearing age range (25 to 34 age group) no doubt tended to increase the correlation between income and education for white females during the time period considered. The reduction in the percentage of white females in this age class was coupled with significant increases in labor force participation by white females, particularly in the older age groups.[3] Both of these changes would tend to increase the degree of the association between income and education for white females. To a lesser extent labor force participation by nonwhite females increased during the same period, which would also tend to increase the degree of association of income and education for this group.

3. See U.S. *Census of Population 1960, Final Report PC(I)-1D,* Table 195.

9

TABLE 2
MEASURES OF THE ASSOCIATION OF INCOME AND YEARS OF SCHOOL COMPLETED IN THE UNITED STATES BY RACE, SEX, AND AGE GROUP, 1949 AND 1959

Race, Sex and Age Group	Mean Income		Mean Years of School Completed		Correlation Coefficient		Regression Coefficient		Standard Error of Estimate	
	1949	1959	1949	1959	1949	1959	1949	1959	1949	1959
White Males	$	$					$	$	$	
25 to 34	3,075	5,436	10.8	11.4	0.25*,a	0.32*,a	175*,d	327*,c	2,108	3,034
35 to 44	3,825	6,531	9.9	10.9	0.35*,a	0.44*,a	345*,d	545*,c	3,134	3,601
45 to 54	3,931	6,186	9.0	9.9	0.35*,a	0.44*,a	380*,d	534*,c	3,610	3,772
55 to 64	3,431	5,421	8.1	8.8	0.32*,a	0.40*,a	314*,d	454*,c	3,487	3,833
Nonwhite Males										
25 to 34	1,745	3,144	7.6	9.3	0.30*,b	0.32*,a	94*,d	182*,c	1,149	1,996
35 to 44	1,838	3,483	6.5	8.2	0.32*,b	0.39*,a	117*,d	241*,c	1,309	2,241
45 to 54	1,768	3,108	5.6	6.7	0.30*,b	0.36*,a	119*,e	213*,c	1,393	2,148
55 to 64	1,524	2,671	5.0	5.6	0.30*,b	0.32*,b	113*,e	187*,c	1,345	2,120
White Females										
25 to 34	1,581	2,296	11.2	11.5	0.20*,a	0.22*,a	99*,d	152*,c	1,375	1,801
35 to 44	1,742	2,511	10.5	11.1	0.21*,a	0.23*,a	113*,d	169*,c	1,727	2,017
45 to 54	1,814	2,753	9.9	10.5	0.23*,a	0.30*,a	133*,d	217*,c	2,005	2,231
55 to 64	1,626	2,411	9.1	9.5	0.23*,a	0.34*,a	130*,d	229*,c	2,144	2,305

TABLE 2 (Continued)

Race, Sex and Age Group	Mean Income		Mean Years of School Completed		Correlation Coefficient		Regression Coefficient		Standard Error of Estimate	
	1949	1959	1949	1959	1949	1959	1949	1959	1949	1959
Nonwhite Females										
25 to 34	965	1,699	8.5	10.0	0.32*,b	0.37*,a	80*,d	161*,c	856	1,355
35 to 44	980	1,746	7.4	8.8	0.33*,b	0.40*,a	88*,d	169*,e	937	1,400
45 to 54	891	1,535	6.3	7.6	0.30*,b	0.40*,b	80*,d	157*,c	955	1,340
55 to 64	771	1,276	5.5	6.3	0.26*,b	0.33*,b	72*,e	117*,e	1,003	1,296

* Significantly different from zero at the 0.01 level. Degrees of freedom determined as being 0.033N in 1949 and 0.05N in 1959, where N = the number of persons reported in the various census tables. Degrees of freedom associated with the various categories vary from 6,811 to 517,286.

a. All differences ≥ 0.02 (approximate) between coefficients with this superscript are statistically significant at the 0.01 level.

b. All differences ≥ 0.04 (approximate) between coefficients with this superscript and a are statistically significant at the 0.01 level.

c. Differences in regression coefficients amounting to $5.00 (approximate) between regression coefficients with this superscript are statistically significant at the 0.01 level.

d. Differences in regression coefficients amounting to $10.00 (approximate) between regression coefficients with this superscript and c are statistically significant at the 0.01 level.

e. Differences in regression coefficients amounting to $15.00 (approximate) between regression coefficients with this superscript and d and c are statistically significant at the 0.01 level.

Source: Same as Table 1 and U.S. Census of Population, 1960, Final Report PC(2)-5B.

TABLE 3

PERCENTAGE OF PERSONS WITH INCOME AGE 25 YEARS AND OLDER
COMPRISING THE SPECIFIED AGE CLASSES BY RACE AND SEX,
1950 AND 1960

Age Group	White Males		Nonwhite Males		White Females		Nonwhite Females	
	1950	1960	1950	1960	1950	1960	1950	1960
25 to 34	27.7	23.2	29.5	26.3	25.6	17.9	31.5	26.0
35 to 44	25.0	24.7	27.5	25.6	23.6	21.3	28.3	25.6
45 to 54	20.1	21.2	21.0	21.0	19.5	20.3	19.6	20.0
55 to 64	15.4	15.7	12.1	14.6	14.3	16.3	9.6	13.5
65 & over	11.8	15.2	9.9	12.5	17.0	24.2	11.0	14.9

Source: Computed from data presented in U.S. Census of Population, 1950, Part I, U.S. Summary, Chapt. C. and U.S. Census of Population, 1960, Final Report PC(1)-1D.

TABLE 4

MEASURES OF THE REGRESSION OF INCOME ON YEARS OF SCHOOL
COMPLETED FOR PERSONS 25 YEARS OF AGE AND OLDER
IN THE UNITED STATES, BY RACE, SEX, AND
YEAR, IN CONSTANT 1957-1959 DOLLARS.*

Year, Race and Sex	Mean Income	Percentage Change in Mean Income from 1949	Regression Coefficient	Percentage Change in Regression Coefficient from 1949
1949	$		$	
White male	4,066		333	
Nonwhite male	2,004		135	
White female	1,910		145	
Nonwhite female	1,071		95	
1959				
White male	5,400	+32.8	454	+36.3
Nonwhite male	2,896	+44.5	208	+54.1
White female	2,191	+14.7	193	+33.1
Nonwhite female	1,464	+36.7	141	+48.4

* Deflated by the Consumer Price Index (1957-59 = 100).
Source: Computed from data presented in the U.S. Census of Population, 1950, Special Report P-E, No. 5B, and U.S. Census of Population, 1960, Final Report PC(1)-1D.

The values in the above analysis are in current dollars. When these values are expressed in constant dollars, it is evident that the persons in the overall classes experienced real gains in mean income and the additional income associated with additional education, although the magnitudes were influenced by the changes in age distribution discussed above (Table 4). The relative gains in mean income and regression coefficients expressed in constant dollars were highest for the nonwhite male class and lowest for white females.

INCOME AND EDUCATION: URBAN-RURAL COMPONENTS OF THE POPULATION

Extensive data on the income and education of the urban-rural components of the population were available for the first time from the 1960 Census of Population. While these tabulations were not so complete as to enable study of the association of income and education for all cross-classifications of persons by age, race, and sex, data were available for all persons 25 years of age and over, and for important subclassifications of residence by age and race.

Mean income, years of school completed, and additional income for additional years of school completed were highest for persons living in urban areas, next highest for rural nonfarm persons, and lowest for the rural farm components of the population for all races and sex classes (Table 5). However, the differences in the measures of the relationship between income and education among the race and sex classes were greater than those within the race and sex groups on the basis of residence. The correlation coefficients were highest in either the urban or rural nonfarm classes and lowest for the rural farm class, where the smallest variation among the race and sex groups was observed. The highest percentages of the variation in income explained by the regression of income on education were for urban and rural nonfarm white

TABLE 5

MEASURES OF THE ASSOCIATION OF INCOME AND YEARS OF SCHOOL COMPLETED FOR PERSONS 25 YEARS OF AGE AND OVER IN THE UNITED STATES, BY URBAN AND RURAL CLASSIFICATION, RACE, AND SEX, 1959

Urban-Rural Classification, Race, and Sex	Mean	Mean Years of School Completed	Correlation Coefficient	Regression Coefficient	Standard Error of Estimate
Urban white male	$5,983	10.4	0.41*,a	$454*,b	$3,709
Rural nonfarm white male	4,584	9.3	0.44*,a	418*,b	3,168
Rural farm white male	3,480	8.6	0.31*,a	305*,b	3,183
Urban nonwhite male	3,314	7.9	0.33*,a	187*,b	2,176
Rural nonfarm nonwhite male	1,936	5.6	0.36*,a	164*,c	1,650
Rural farm nonwhite male	1,326	4.7	0.28*,a	128*,b	1,469
Urban white female	2,380	10.2	0.31*,a	200*,b	2,158
Rural nonfarm white female	1,758	9.7	0.33*,a	167*,b	1,703
Rural farm white female	1,566	9.5	0.31*,a	151*,b	1,655
Urban nonwhite female	1,646	8.4	0.38*,a	144*,b	1,385
Rural nonfarm nonwhite female	923	6.3	0.37*,a	94*,b	957
Rural farm nonwhite female	767	5.9	0.31*,a	71*,b	826

* Significantly different from zero at the 0.01 level. Degrees of freedom determined as being 0.25N, where N = the number of persons reported in the respective census tables. Degrees of freedom associated with the various categories vary from 4,454 to 7,335,930.

  a. All differences ≥ 0.02 (approximate) are statistically significant at the 0.01 level.

  b. Differences amounting to $5.00 (approximate) between regression coefficients with this superscript are statistically significant at the 0.01 level.

  c. Differences amounting to $10.00 (approximate) between regression coefficient with this superscript and b are statistically significant at the 0.01 level.

Source: Same as Table 1.

males, and for the same residence groupings of nonwhite females. Most of the differences within and between the cross-classifications were statistically significant.

The major classifications for which detailed information was available for analysis of the association of income and education for males by race and age were the Central Cities of Urban Areas and Rural Farm categories. The form in which Census data were tabulated precluded a comparative racial analysis for the other major categories.

The mean incomes and educational achievement of males in the Central Cities were consistently above those of their Rural Farm counterparts (Table 6). The closest parallels in terms of both incomes and years of school completed were between Central Cities nonwhite males and Rural Farm white males, where the age patterns of both income and education were quite similar. The mean incomes of Central Cities white males were substantially above those in the other categories except in the youngest age groups, and the mean incomes and educational achievements of Rural Farm nonwhite males were considerably below those of the other classes. For all categories, maximum mean incomes were realized in the 35 to 44 age class, and excepting Central Cities white males, the highest mean years of school completed occurred in the 20 to 21 age group.

The correlation and regression coefficients tended to exhibit the same age pattern as did the mean incomes, with the same type of differences among racial and residence classes (Table 7). The correlation coefficients for Central Cities nonwhite males in general followed the same pattern by age as for Rural Farm white males with differences which were typically not statistically significant. However, the regression coefficients for Rural Farm white males were substantially greater than those for the Central Cities nonwhite males. Again, both the variation in income "explained" by

TABLE 6

MEAN INCOMES AND YEARS OF SCHOOL COMPLETED FOR MALES IN THE CENTRAL CITIES OF URBAN AREAS AND FOR RURAL FARM MALES, BY RACE AND AGE, 1959

Age Group	MEAN INCOME		MEAN YEARS OF SCHOOL COMPLETED		MEAN INCOME		MEAN YEARS OF SCHOOL COMPLETED	
	Central Cities White Males	Central Cities Nonwhite Males	Central Cities White Males	Central Cities Nonwhite Males	Rural Farm White Males	Rural Farm Nonwhite Males	Rural Farm White Males	Rural Farm Nonwhite Males
25 & Over	$5656	$3491	10.1	8.2	$3534	$1330	8.6	4.7
14 & 15	953	1218	8.3	7.8	898	684	8.0	6.1
16 & 17	878	1029	9.8	9.3	799	685	9.5	7.3
18 & 19	1522	1390	11.2	10.2	1271	826	10.3	7.8
20 & 21	2484	2060	11.7	10.6	2082	946	10.7	7.8
22 to 24	3468	2608	11.9	10.4	2655	1187	10.5	7.2
25 to 29	4877	3382	12.0	10.3	3447	1324	10.2	6.5
30 to 34	6065	3744	11.5	9.7	4042	1500	10.0	5.9
35 to 44	6764	3958	11.2	9.0	4268	1586	9.5	5.2
45 to 54	6744	3699	10.2	7.5	3888	1430	8.6	4.6
55 to 64	6140	3259	9.1	6.4	3326	1211	7.8	4.0
65 to 74	3793	2102	7.7	5.4	2347	997	7.2	3.6
75 & Over	2531	1421	7.3	4.8	1765	815	6.7	3.4

Source: Computed from data presented in *U.S. Census of Population, 1960, Final Report* PC (2)-5B.

the regression and the additional income per additional year of school completed were considerably lower for the Rural Farm nonwhite males than for the other categories.

INCOME AND EDUCATION: MALES BY REGION, RACE AND AGE

It is possible to construct the income and education distributions for males by race and age in the South and Nonsouth areas of the United States for both 1949 and 1959.

The Association of Income and Education, 1949. — In 1949, mean incomes generally increased with age for whites through the 45 to 54 age group (Table 8). On the other hand, income increased with age for nonwhites through the 35 to 44 age group. The highest mean years of school completed for Nonsouth white males was associated with the 25 to 29 age group, that for Nonsouth nonwhite males in the 20 to 21 year age group, for South white males in the 22 to 24 and 25 to 29 year classes, and for South nonwhite males in the 20 and 21 year old classes. The distributions of mean education by age illustrate the increasing level of education of succeeding generations, and also the lag in educational achievement for nonwhites, in particular, and South white males.

The correlation between income and education in 1949 was low, but statistically significant, for all major groups, and was higher for males in the South than for their Nonsouth counterparts (Table 9). In the youngest age classes, both the correlation coefficients and the regression coefficients were generally not significantly different from zero, and tended to be negative. Both the correlation coefficients and the regression coefficients increased with age at least through the age 30 to 34 group. The maximum additional income for an additional year of school completed was in

TABLE 7

Specified Measures of the Association of Income and Years of School Completed for Males in the Central Cities of Urban Areas and for Rural Farm Males, by Race and Age, 1959

Age Group	Correlation Coefficients		Regression Coefficients		Correlation Coefficients		Regression Coefficients	
	Central Cities White Males	Central Cities Nonwhite Males	Central Cities White Males	Central Cities Nonwhite Males	Rural Farm White Males	Rural Farm Nonwhite Males	Rural Farm White Males	Rural Farm Nonwhite Males
25 & Over	.36*,a	.29*,a	$438*,c	$174*,c	.30*,a	.28*,b	$326*,c	$139*,d
14 & 15	−.04*,b	−.09*	−33*,d	−67*	−.05*	−.00	−36*	−0
16 & 17	−.02	−.04	−18	−27	−.02	−.01	−14	−2
18 & 19	−.08*,b	−.02	−60*,d	−14	.08*	.09*	46*	27*
20 & 21	−.12*,b	−.02	−94*,d	−10	.15*	.07	99*	18
22 to 24	−.00	.07*	−0	42*	.21*	.21*	161*	73*
25 to 29	.18*,a	.18*,b	161*,c	108*,d	.24*,b	.29*	245*	98*
30 to 34	.34*,a	.27*,b	380*,d	165*,d	.26*,b	.28*	301*	127*
35 to 44	.38*,a	.28*,b	536*,c	188*,c	.28*,b	.34*	349*	212*
45 to 54	.39*,a	.27*,b	566*,c	174*,d	.28*,b	.30*	350*,c	165*
55 to 64	.35*,a	.25*,b	476*,d	154*,d	.27*,b	.18*	316*	89*
65 to 74	.31*,a	.24*,b	325*,c	128*,d	.24*,b	.19*	210*,c	64*
75 & Over	.28*,a	.23*	243*,d	101*	.20*	.21*	154*	49*

18

TABLE 7 (*Continued*)

* Significantly different from zero at the 0.01 level. Degrees of freedom were 0.05N for the respective categories and varied from 732 to 654,041.

a. All differences $\geq$ 0.02 (approximate) between coefficients with this superscript are statistically significant at the 0.01 level.

b. All differences $\geq$ 0.04 (approximate) between coefficients with this superscript and a are statistically significant at the 0.01 level.

c. Differences amounting to $15.00 (approximate) between regression coefficients with this superscript are statistically significant at the 0.01 level.

d. Differences amounting to $20.00 (approximate) between regression coefficients with this superscript and c are statistically significant at the 0.01 level.

e. Differences amounting to $25.00 (approximate) between regression coefficients with this superscript and d and c are statistically significant at the 0.01 level.

Source: Same as Table 6.

TABLE 8
MEAN INCOMES AND YEARS OF SCHOOL COMPLETED FOR MALES BY AGE, REGION, AND RACE, 1949

	MEAN INCOME				MEAN YEARS OF SCHOOL COMPLETED			
Age Group	Nonsouth White Males	Nonsouth Nonwhite Males	South White Males	South Nonwhite Males	Nonsouth White Males	Nonsouth Nonwhite Males	South White Males	South Nonwhite Males
25 & Over	$3520	$2229	$2948	$1303	9.6	7.6	8.7	5.3
14 & 15	480	471	386	313	9.4	6.9	7.1	5.5
16 & 17	421	531	467	431	9.0	8.8	8.3	6.4
18 & 19	974	931	871	665	10.7	9.4	9.5	7.0
20 & 21	1615	1421	1373	946	11.1	9.6	9.9	7.2
22 to 24	2178	1826	1886	1180	11.2	9.5	10.0	7.0
25 to 29	2888	2112	2517	1368	11.3	9.4	10.0	6.7
30 to 34	3509	2362	3024	1465	11.0	8.9	9.7	6.3
35 to 44	4006	2396	3327	1481	10.3	8.0	9.0	5.5
45 to 54	4106	2323	3385	1410	9.2	6.9	8.3	4.7
55 to 64	3569	2124	2941	1181	8.2	6.3	7.7	4.2
65 to 74	2415	1548	1972	747	7.6	5.6	7.0	3.6
75 & Over	1566	965	1352	502	7.4	4.7	6.6	2.9

Source: Same as Table 1.

the age 45 to 54 class for Nonsouth males and South white males. There were substantial differences in the degree of the association of income and education and the regression coefficients among the races.

The Association of Income and Education, 1959. — Between 1949 and 1959 the absolute differences in mean incomes increased among the race and regional groups, although the percentage increases in mean incomes were higher in the South and for nonwhites than for Nonsouth white males (Table 10).[4] The highest mean incomes for all groups were in the age 35 to 44 classes. This suggests that for white males the maximum mean incomes were received at an earlier age than in 1949. While the differences in mean incomes between race and region increased, the absolute differences in educational achievement narrowed. The highest mean educational achievement existed in essentially the same age groups in 1959 as in 1949.

The correlation and regression coefficients increased substantially for all groups from 1949 to 1959 (Table 11). The absolute differences in regression coefficients increased, and in fact those of Nonsouth white males increased more than those of white males in the South, both in percentage and in absolute terms. Again, both the degree of the association and the additional income for additional school years varied with age. Most of the differences among racial and regional groups were statistically significant.

As indicated earlier, functions which were linear in logarithms of income were also fitted to the income and education data. In the case of the regional data, the results were such as to indicate that the percentage variation of income with edu-

4. The 1959 data on the association of income and education by region and race are taken from my article "The Association of Income and Education for Males by Region, Race, and Age," *The Southern Economic Journal,* July, 1965, pp. 15-22.

21

TABLE 9

SPECIFIED MEASURES OF THE ASSOCIATION OF INCOME AND YEARS OF SCHOOL COMPLETED FOR MALES BY AGE, REGION, AND RACE, 1949

Age Group	CORRELATION COEFFICIENTS				REGRESSION COEFFICIENTS			
	Nonsouth White Males	Nonsouth Nonwhite Males	South White Males	South Nonwhite Males	Nonsouth White Males	Nonsouth Nonwhite Males	South White Males	South Nonwhite Males
25 & Over	.28*,a	.19*,a	.36*,a	.30*,a	$264*,c	$ 74*,c	$289*,c	$ 93*,c
14 & 15	−.06*,b	.03	.02	.02	−25*,d	9	6	3
16 & 17	.01	−.01	−.02	−.03	4	−4	−6	−5
18 & 19	−.09*,b	−.01	.00	.04	−37*,c	−3	0	6
20 & 21	−.08*,b	.05	.08*,b	.08*	−38*,c	19	28*,c	19*,d
22 to 24	−.01	.08*	.16*,b	.16*	−5	31*	62*,c	40*,c
25 to 29	.15*,a	.10*	.29*,a	.25*,b	96*,c	35*,d	142*,c	66*,c
30 to 34	.26*,a	.17*	.39*,a	.31*,b	223*,c	71*,e	260*,c	84*,c
35 to 44	.32*,a	.20*,b	.40*,a	.28*,b	340*,c	82*,d	341*,c	93*,c
45 to 54	.33*,a	.22*,b	.38*,b	.25*,b	371*,c	91*,d	387*,d	92*,c
55 to 64	.31*,a	.20*	.32*,b	.25*	300*,c	83*,e	347*,d	88*,d
65 to 74	.27*,a	.20*	.27*	.23*	224*,c	85*	255*,d	57*,c
75 & Over	.24*,b	.20*		.15*	176*,d	51*	176*	21*,c

* Significantly different from zero at the 0.01 level. Degrees of freedom determined as being 0.033N, and varied from 197 to 826,990.

TABLE 9 (*Continued*)

a. All differences $\geq$ 0.02 (approximate) between coefficients with this superscript are statistically significant at the 0.01 level.

b. All differences $\geq$ 0.04 (approximate) between coefficients with this superscript and a are statistically significant at the 0.01 level.

c. Differences amounting to $15.00 (approximate) between regression coefficients with this superscript are statistically significant at the 0.01 level.

d. Differences amounting to $20.00 (approximate) between regression coefficients with this superscript and c are statistically significant at the 0.01 level.

e. Differences amounting to $25.00 (approximate) between regression coefficients with this superscript and d and c are statistically significant at the 0.01 level.

Source: Same as Table 1.

23

cation was higher in the South than for the Nonsouth. The correlation coefficients for the logarithmic functions were only slightly lower for South males than those derived from the arithmetic functions (Table 12). On the other hand, the correlation coefficients associated with the logarithmic functions for Nonsouth males were appreciably lower than for the arithmetic relationships, except for the very youngest and oldest age groups. It would appear that educational achievement is a better explanation of the relative variation in income in the South than for the Nonsouth.

TABLE 10
Mean Incomes and Years of School Completed for Males by Age, Region, and Race, 1959

Age Group	Mean Income				Mean Years of School Completed			
	Nonsouth White Males	Nonsouth Nonwhite Males	South White Males	South Nonwhite Males	Nonsouth White Males	Nonsouth Nonwhite Males	South White Males	South Nonwhite Males
25 & Over	$5831	$3790	$4926	$2183	10.2	8.5	9.5	6.2
14 & 15	897	1183	943	846	8.2	7.8	7.7	6.7
16 & 17	836	1006	841	793	9.8	9.4	9.3	8.1
18 & 19	1470	1409	1273	998	11.1	10.4	10.6	9.0
20 & 21	2503	2122	2087	1397	11.7	10.7	11.1	9.3
22 to 24	3542	2689	2980	1803	11.8	10.7	11.2	9.0
25 to 29	5032	3598	4280	2278	11.8	10.6	11.1	8.6
30 to 34	6216	4048	5383	2547	11.5	10.1	10.8	7.9
35 to 44	6902	4350	5883	2589	11.2	9.3	10.3	7.0
45 to 54	6703	4015	5492	2351	10.2	7.8	9.2	5.8
55 to 64	5896	3538	4800	1935	9.0	6.7	8.3	4.7
65 to 74	3505	2229	2977	1291	7.8	5.8	7.5	3.8
75 & Over	2198	1487	1910	889	7.3	5.1	6.8	3.4

Source: Same as Table 6.

25

TABLE 11

Specified Measures of the Association of Income and Years of School Completed for Males by Age, Region, and Race, 1959

Age Groups	Correlation Coefficients				Regression Coefficients			
	Nonsouth White Males	Nonsouth Nonwhite Males	South White Males	South Nonwhite Males	Nonsouth White Males	Nonsouth Nonwhite Males	South White Males	South Nonwhite Males
25 & Over	.38*,a	.28*,a	.43*,a	.36*,a	$492*,c	$186*,c	$473*,c	$162*,c
14 & 15	-.04*,b	-.12*	-.05*,b	.02	-28*,a	-91*	-35*	11
16 & 17	-.02	-.01	-.01	.00	-18	-5	-8	1
18 & 19	-.04*,a	-.02	-.02*	.03	-32*,c	-13	-12*,c	11
20 & 21	-.09*,a	-.02	-.00	.07*	-76*,c	-11	-2	25*,d
22 to 24	.02*,a	.06*	.13*,b	.17*,b	20*,c	38*	89*,e	65*,d
25 to 29	.20*,a	.17*,b	.32*,a	.28*,b	189*,c	109*,c	243*,c	114*,c
30 to 34	.34*,a	.27*,b	.42*,a	.35*,b	411*,c	190*,c	417*,c	152*,c
35 to 44	.39*,a	.28*,b	.46*,a	.36*,b	589*,c	218*,d	541*,c	172*,c
45 to 54	.40*,a	.26*,b	.45*,a	.34*,b	611*,c	184*,d	573*,c	170*,c
55 to 64	.36*,a	.23*,b	.42*,a	.29*,b	517*,c	154*,e	525*,d	141*,c
65 to 74	.31*,a	.21*	.36*,a	.24*,b	331*,c	114*,e	356*,d	108*,d
75 & Over	.26*,a	.17*	.30*,b	.21*	216*,c	74*	237*,c	73*,d

* Significantly different from zero at the 0.01 level. Degrees of freedom determined as being 0.05N and varied from 1,070 to 1,541,950.

TABLE 11 (*Continued*)

a. All differences ≥ 0.02 (approximate) between coefficients with this superscript are significant at the 0.01 level.

b. All differences ≥ 0.04 (approximate) between coefficients with this superscript and a are statistically significant at the 0.01 level.

c. Differences amounting to $15.00 (approximate) between regression coefficients with this superscript are statistically significant at the 0.01 level.

d. Differences amounting to $20.00 (approximate) between regression coefficients with this superscript and c are statistically significant at the 0.01 level.

e. Differences amounting to $25.00 (approximate) between regression coefficients with this superscript and d and c are statistically significant at the 0.01 level.

Source: Same as Table 6.

TABLE 12
Correlation Coefficients Relating Income and Education as Derived from Specified Functions for Males by Age, Region, and Race, 1959

	Y = a + bX Correlation Coefficient				logY = a + bX Correlation Coefficient			
Age Group	Nonsouth White Males	Nonsouth Nonwhite Males	South White Males	South Nonwhite Males	Nonsouth White Males	Nonsouth Nonwhite Males	South White Males	South Nonwhite Males
25 & Over	.38	.28	.43	.36	.34	.24	.42	.33
14 & 15	−.04	−.11	−.05	.02	−.05	−.12	−.04	.01
16 & 17	−.02	−.01	−.01	.00	−.02	−.02	−.03	−.02
18 & 19	−.04	−.02	−.02	.03	−.02	−.01	−.02	.01
20 & 21	−.09	−.02	−.00	.07	−.12	−.01	−.03	.06
22 to 24	.02	.06	.13	.17	−.01	.06	.11	.16
25 to 29	.20	.17	.32	.28	.16	.13	.29	.24
30 to 34	.34	.27	.42	.35	.27	.20	.38	.28
35 to 44	.39	.28	.46	.36	.31	.20	.40	.29
45 to 54	.40	.26	.45	.34	.28	.17	.38	.25
55 to 64	.36	.23	.42	.29	.24	.18	.36	.22
65 to 74	.31	.21	.36	.24	.24	.17	.36	.23
75 & Over	.26	.17	.30	.21	.24	.19	.36	.22

Source: Same as Table 6.

3. PRIVATE INCENTIVES
TO INVEST IN EDUCATION

O ne approach to measuring the "value" of education, and thus the varying incentives among groups, is to determine the total income over a period of years associated with different levels of educational achievement.[1] The examples employed here are for 8, 12, and 16 years of school completed, and assume zero income until completion of the specified number of school years.[2] These incomes were computed from the year in which the given year of school would normally be completed through age 64, and were determined as follows: (1) the regression equations for each age group were employed to estimate the annual income within age groups for the various years of school completed; (2) the annual incomes were multiplied by the number of years included in the age group to determine total incomes for that number of years, and (3) the total incomes in each age group were summed to give the estimates of income from completion of the specified years of school through age 64.[3] This procedure allows for changes in income with age and variation in the additional income associated with additional schooling over the age span.

Income for Males in the Central Cities and Rural Farm Areas, 1959. — The total incomes received by males from

1. This is the approach of Miller, "Annual and Lifetime Income," pp. 979-84.
2. It should be noted that in neither the lifetime incomes estimated nor the rates of return which are presented in the following section is there a "correction" for unemployment. The Census data include all those who received income during the year, and thus the mean is influenced by the low incomes of those who were employed less than the full year.
3. No adjustment was made to these estimates for varying life expectancies as the life expectancy of the "average" person in these categories was at least through age 65 (see *Statistical Abstract of the United States,* 1963, p. 60).

completion of 8 years of school to age 65 ranged from $229 thousand for white males in the Central Cities to $83 thousand for Rural Farm nonwhite males (Table 13). At this level of education, the incomes of Central Cities nonwhite males exceeded those of Rural Farm white males. As the level of education increased, the differences between the incomes of Central Cities white males and those of the other categories increased to 12 years of school completed, and then de-

TABLE 13

TOTAL INCOME OF MALES FROM THE YEAR OF ESTIMATED SPECIFIED YEARS OF SCHOOL COMPLETED THROUGH AGE 64 IN THE CENTRAL CITIES OF URBAN AREAS AND RURAL FARM AREAS BY RACE, 1959

Years of School Completed	Central Cities White Males	Central Cities Nonwhite Males	Rural Farm White Males	Rural Farm Nonwhite Males
8	$229,000[a]	$161,000[a]	$155,000[a]	$ 83,000[a]
12	297,000[b]	182,000[b]	206,000[b]	104,000[b]
16	310,000[c]	201,000[c]	250,000[c]	123,000[c]

a. Assumes that eight years of school are completed in the year that the person is 14 years of age.
b. Assumes that twelve years of school are completed in the year that the person is 18 years of age.
c. Assumes that sixteen years of school are completed in the year that the person is 22 years of age.
Source: Same as Table 6.

creased. There were noticeable income advantages associated with higher educational achievements. However, the differences in incomes for nonwhites by level of education were considerably smaller than those for whites.

Income for Males in the South and Nonsouth Areas, 1949. There were substantial income advantages associated with increased levels of education for all groups in 1949, although these advantages were most pronounced for white males (Table 14). Differences between incomes of South and Non-

30

south white males were rather small for all levels of education, and tended to decline with increased educational achievement. On the other hand, differences between the incomes of whites and nonwhites were considerable and these differences increased with the level of education. Nonsouth nonwhite males had a significant income advantage over their counterparts in the South.

TABLE 14

ESTIMATED TOTAL INCOME OF MALES FROM THE YEAR OF
SPECIFIED YEARS OF SCHOOL COMPLETED THROUGH
AGE 64 BY REGION AND RACE, 1949

Years of School Completed	Nonsouth White Males	Nonsouth Nonwhite Males	South White Males	South Nonwhite Males
8	$145,000[a]	$104,000[a]	$127,000[a]	$73,000[a]
12	189,000[b]	115,000[b]	178,000[b]	85,000[b]
16	229,000[c]	121,000[c]	224,000[c]	96,000[c]

a. Assumes that eight years of school are completed in the year that the person is 14 years of age.
b. Assumes that twelve years of school are completed in the year that the person is 18 years of age.
c. Assumes that sixteen years of school are completed in the year that the person is 22 years of age.
Source: Same as Table 6.

There are differences in the income estimates derived by the regression technique and other available estimates. For example, H. P. Miller's estimates for 1949 for whites and nonwhites in the United States deviate from the regression estimates, even when these are weighted by their respective frequencies (Table 15).[4] The regression estimates appear to overstate the income associated with 8 and 12 years of school completed for white males and understate the income

4. Miller's estimates were derived by calculating the mean income for each census class of years of school completed and employing these means to derive the total income estimates. See "Annual and Lifetime Income," pp. 979-84, for a discussion of his procedures.

31

TABLE 15

ESTIMATES OF INCOME OF MALES FROM AGE 18 THROUGH 64 AS DETERMINED BY REGRESSION TECHNIQUE AND BY MILLER, FOR SPECIFIED YEARS OF SCHOOL COMPLETED BY RACE, 1949

Year of School Completed	REGRESSION ESTIMATE[a]		MILLER'S ESTIMATE[b]	REGRESSION ESTIMATE[a]		MILLER'S ESTIMATE[b]
	Nonsouth White Males	South White Males	U.S. White Males	Nonsouth Nonwhite Males	South Nonwhite Males	U.S. Nonwhite Males
8	$143,000	$125,000	$119,000	$102,000	$ 71,000	$ 71,000
12	189,000	178,000	162,000	115,000	85,000	85,000
16	241,000[c]	236,000[c]	255,000	129,000[c]	102,000[c]	117,000

a. Adjusted to reflect Miller's assumptions.

b. Obtained from, H. P. Miller, "Income and Education: Does Education Pay Off?," *Economics of Higher Education*, ed. Selma J. Mushkin, U.S. Department of Health, Education and Welfare, OE, 50027, Bul. 1962, No. 5, page 140.

c. Miller's estimates were for completion of 16 years of school and over. This figure was derived by assuming that the mean years of school completed by persons completing at least 16 years of school was 16.5 years.

32

associated with college education. On the other hand, if the incomes of nonwhite males in South and Nonsouth were weighted by their respective frequencies, there would be less deviation between the regression estimates and those of Miller.

Income for Males in the South and Nonsouth Areas, 1959.[5] The incomes of all regional and racial groups were higher

TABLE 16

ESTIMATED TOTAL INCOME OF MALES FROM THE YEAR OF SPECIFIED
NUMBER OF YEARS OF SCHOOL COMPLETED THROUGH
AGE 64 BY REGION AND RACE, 1959

Years of School Completed	Nonsouth White Males	Nonsouth Nonwhite Males	South White Males	South Nonwhite Males
8	$224,000[a]	$172,000[a]	$197,000[a]	$115,000[a]
12	300,000[b]	195,000[b]	274,000[b]	138,000[b]
16	371,000[c]	215,000[c]	346,000[c]	157,000[c]

a. Assumes that eight years of school are completed in the year that the person is 14 years of age.
b. Assumes that twelve years of school are completed in the year that the person is 18 years of age.
c. Assumes that sixteen years of school are completed in the year that the person is 22 years of age.
Source: Same as Table 6.

for each of the specified years of school completed in 1959 (Table 16). Furthermore, the income advantages of a high school or college education were more pronounced in 1959 than in 1949. There were wide differentials in income in 1959 by region and race, which were greater than those of 1949. Again the differences in income among the groups in-

5. Part of the discussion of incomes by race and region in this section and rates of return to education in the following section is based on my article, "The Association of Income and Education for Males by Region, Race, and Age," *The Southern Economic Journal,* July, 1965, pp. 15-22.

creased with education, excepting Nonsouth and South white males. However, the differences between these two groups were greater in 1959 than in 1949, and did not narrow as rapidly with increased educational attainment. Nonwhites in both regions had the greatest relative improvement in income, but the absolute differences between the races increased. Unfortunately, there are no available alternative income estimates for the 1959 data to compare with the regression estimates for the same year.

When the incomes in 1949 and 1959 associated with various years of school completed are standardized in terms of dollars of constant purchasing power, it is evident that all groups experienced substantial increases in real income (Table 17).

RATES OF RETURN TO INVESTMENT IN EDUCATION OVER COST

The differences in income as derived from the income-age profile data above are not directly indicative of differences in private incentives to invest in education, in that the costs to individuals of obtaining additional education are ignored. Economic incentives must be measured in terms of both costs and rewards. Therefore, the possibility of different private incentives to invest in education among groups was explored by computing internal rates of return over opportunity costs (the income foregone while attending school). These internal rates of return were estimated as follows: (1) the regression coefficients for the various age groups were employed as estimates of the additional income attributed to the marginal year of school completed as an individual would pass through succeeding age groups in his life span; (2) the life expectancies of white and nonwhite males of ages appropriate to the specified educational achievement were used to determine the number of years over which the added incomes would

TABLE 17
Estimated Total Income of Males from the Year of Specified Years of School completed through age 64 in Constant 1957-59 Dollars by Region and Race, 1949-59*

Years of School Completed	Nonsouth White Males		Nonsouth Nonwhite Males		South White Males		South Nonwhite Males	
	1949	1959	1949	1959	1949	1959	1949	1959
8	$175,000	$221,000	$125,000	$169,000	$153,000	$194,000	$ 88,000	$113,000
12	228,000	296,000	139,000	192,000	214,000	270,000	102,000	136,000
16	276,000	366,000	146,000	212,000	270,000	341,000	111,000	155,000

* Deflated by the Index of Consumer Prices (1957-59 = 100).
Source: Computed from data in Tables 14 and 16

accrue;[6] (3) the opportunity costs to individuals were estimated by employing the regression equations appropriate to the age groups in which the specified years of school would be undertaken to derive the income associated with one year of school completed less than the marginal years; and (4) the rates of discount which equated the present values of additional income to opportunity costs were determined by an iterative computer technique.[7] No attempt was made to adjust the added lifetime incomes for different employment rates, nor was there any explicit recognition of costs other than opportunity costs. Costs, other than opportunity costs, were not initially employed because Schultz and others have shown that opportunity costs are the most significant element of private costs.[8] In the discussion of the rates of return to a four-year college education in 1959, tuition and fee costs are introduced so as to evaluate the regional and racial variations in these costs as they influence the rates of return to a college education. All rates of return were determined on added incomes before federal income taxes, and thus are somewhat greater than the net rates of return to education.[9]

Determination of rates of return over all costs, including

6. The life expectancies for white and nonwhite males is given in *Statistical Abstract of the United States*, 1963. The ages for the respective years of school were determined in the same manner as in Tables 14 & 16.

7. Specifically the internal rate of return is the value of r in the following expression:

$$C = \sum_{i=1}^{n} \frac{b_i}{(1+r)^i}$$

where: C = the opportunity cost
n = the life expectancy
b_i = the added income in the ith year
r = the rate of discount.

8. See Schultz, "Capital Formation by Education," p. 580; Hansen, "Total and Private Rates," pp. 130, 131.

9. Based on 1949 data, Hansen found that allowance for federal income taxes reduced the rates of return one to two percentage points. See "Total and Private Rates," p. 136.

society's contribution to the educational process, was beyond the scope of this study. However, it should be recognized that inclusion of these costs would reduce the rates of return to education from those presented. Furthermore, the reduction in rates of return for the South would be relatively less than in those for the Nonsouth because of the generally lower per student expenditures for education in the South.

The procedure followed does have the limitation of attaching equal monetary significance to each additional year of school for the specified age category. However, it does give weight to the rising and differential opportunity costs with age and education, the influence of the time shape of the increment to income, and the reduced life expectancies associated with the ages at which higher levels of educational achievement takes place.

Rates of Return on Education for Males in the Central Cities and Rural Farm Males, 1959. — As might be expected, there were considerable differences in the rates of return to males in the various residence and racial groupings (Table 18). However, the rankings of the rates of return were considerably different from those which might be indicated from the total incomes of the previous section. The returns to the educational investment were higher for Rural Farm males than for their Central Cities counterparts. The primary reason for this phenomenon is found in the considerably lower opportunity costs to Rural Farm males which more than offset the differentials in additional incomes for additional year of school completed. The investment in education by nonwhites was less attractive than that of white males, although the differences in rates of return between Central Cities white males and Rural Farm nonwhite males were small.

Rates of Return on Education for Males in the South and

TABLE 18

INTERNAL RATES OF RETURN OVER OPPORTUNITY COST FOR COMPLETION
OF SPECIFIED YEAR OF SCHOOL FOR MALES IN THE CENTRAL CITIES
OF URBAN AREAS AND FOR RURAL FARM MALES BY RACE, 1959

	RATES OF RETURN FOR:*			
Region and Race	10th Year	12th Year	13th Year	16th Year
Central Cities White Males	12	10	11	8
Central Cities Nonwhite Males	7	6	7	4
Rural Farm White Males	15	13	14	8
Rural Farm Nonwhite Males	11	10	10	7

* Rates of return are rounded to the nearest whole percentage point.
Source: Same as Table 6.

TABLE 19

INTERNAL RATES OF RETURN OVER OPPORTUNITY COST FOR COMPLETION
OF SPECIFIED YEAR OF SCHOOL FOR MALES BY REGION AND RACE, 1949

	RATES OF RETURN FOR:*			
Region and Race	10th Year	12th Year	13th Year	16th Year
Nonsouth White Males	13	10	11	8
Nonsouth Nonwhite Males	7	5	5	2
South White Males	16	13	14	9
South Nonwhite Males	10	8	8	4

* Rates of return are rounded to the nearest whole percentage point.
Source: Same as Table 6.

TABLE 20

INTERNAL RATES OF RETURN OVER OPPORTUNITY COST FOR COMPLETION
OF SPECIFIED YEAR OF SCHOOL FOR MALES BY REGION AND RACE, 1959

	RATES OF RETURN FOR*			
Region and Race	10th Year	12th Year	13th Year	16th Year
Nonsouth White Males	13	12	13	9
Nonsouth Nonwhite Males	8	8	8	5
South White Males	15	14	15	10
South Nonwhite Males	10	9	10	6

* Rates of return are rounded to the nearest whole percentage point.
Source: Same as Table 6.

38

Nonsouth, 1949. — South white males received the highest rate of return on the educational investment, and the rates of return to education for South nonwhite males were above their Nonsouth counterparts (Table 19). Again the differences in opportunity costs played a significant role, and more than offset regional differences in the additional income associated with additional school. Racial differences in rates of return were substantial and were attributable to relatively small differences in opportunity costs and substantial racial differences in the regression coefficients.

Rates of Return on Education for Males in the South and Nonsouth, 1959. — Regional and racial differences in rates of return on the educational investment persisted in 1959, although these differences narrowed somewhat in 1959 as contrasted to 1949 (Table 20). Specifically, the differences between South males and Nonsouth males narrowed, indicating a relative improvement in returns to education for Nonsouth males. The racial differences in rates of return were smaller in 1959 than in 1949.

A comparison of the rates of return for all groups in 1949 and 1959 indicates that these rates were not depressed by the higher number and proportion of persons with increased levels of education attained (again see Tables 19 and 20). In fact, the rates of return were higher in 1959 for all groups and levels of education, excepting those completing the 10th year of school. This suggests that the secular growth of the economy was great enough to offset the marginal effects of increased educational attainment. The greatest improvement in rates of return to education, in both relative and absolute terms, was for Nonsouth nonwhite males.

Rates of Return on College Education in the South and Nonsouth, 1959. — The previous analysis dealt with rates of return over opportunity cost for the specified marginal years of school completed and ignored other cost items. While these other costs are negligible for the high school years and may be omitted in a first approximation of the differences in private incentives to invest in higher education, the possibilities of regional and racial differences in these costs as they apply to college education cannot be ignored.

Elements of Cost for a Four-Year College Education. — In determining the total opportunity costs for four years of college education, the regression equations were employed to estimate what a person of the specified age would earn with one year of education less than the one in question for each of the four years of college. The sum of the opportunity costs for the individual years was used as the total opportunity cost of obtaining a college education.

The tuition and fee costs were estimated by employing data from a study of annual cost of college education by the Life Insurance Agency Management Association for 1960-61 at 950 colleges and universities.[10] The report on this study gave the name of the institution, its location, whether it was public or private, the undergraduate enrollment, and the significant cost items. Weighted average tuition and fee costs were computed by using male enrollments as the weights for the following categories of institutions: (1) Nonsouth private colleges; (2) Nonsouth public colleges; (3) South white private colleges; (4) South white public colleges; (5) South Negro private colleges; and (6) South Negro public colleges. The traditional Negro colleges were identified from a standard listing of American colleges.[11] It was assumed that nonwhites outside the South had the same tuition and fee costs

10. *The Cost of Four Years of College* (distributed by the New York Life Insurance Company).
11. Specifically, James Cass and Max Birnbaum, *Comparative Guide to American Colleges*, New York, Harper, 1964.

as whites. Within the South the tuition and fee costs for whites were assumed to be those of the traditionally white colleges and universities, and these costs for nonwhites were assumed to be those of the traditionally Negro colleges.[12]

Room, board, and other living costs were not included in the cost of education because these costs would have existed irrespective of attendance at college, although they would not necessarily have been of the same magnitude nor borne by the same person.

When the cost estimates for four years of college are tabulated, the major significance of opportunity costs is apparent (Table 21). There are considerable differences between regions in tuition and fee costs, particularly for the private colleges and universities. Within the South there are major differences in costs between races in all the groups. South nonwhite males have the lowest opportunity costs and the lowest tuition and fee costs. In spite of somewhat higher opportunity costs, the total cost of college for South white males is below that of Nonsouth nonwhite males because of the markedly lower tuition and fee costs.

Rates of Return on a Four-Year College Education. — The increments to lifetime income resulting from a college education were estimated using the regression equations, following the procedure described at the beginning of this section. The costs of the investment were taken to be the combination of opportunity costs and tuition and fee costs, and the rates of return were computed on these costs. Technically, the educational investment is made over a four-year period, and interest costs should be added to reflect the interest foregone in making the educational investment. However, the interest charges were not added to costs in computing the rates of return be-

12. This was considered a reasonable assumption in that there was no significant integration in higher education in the South for the year in question.

41

TABLE 21

Major Costs of Obtaining a Four-Year College Education for Males by Region, Race, and Type of Institution, 1960-61.

Region and Race	Opportunity Cost	Tuition and Fees			Total of Costs		
		Private College	Public College	Average of Private and Public Colleges	Private College	Public College	Average of Private and Public Colleges
Nonsouth White Male	$9,791	$3,488	$948	$2,128	$13,279	$10,739	$11,919
Nonsouth Nonwhite Male[a]	8,418	3,488	948	2,128	11,906	9,366	10,546
South White Male	8,735	2,428	722	1,228	11,163	9,457	9,973
South Nonwhite Male[b]	6,213	1,416	680	968	7,629	6,893	7,181

a. Nonsouth nonwhite males were assumed to attend the same institutions as white males.

b. South nonwhite males were assumed to attend all-Negro or traditionally Negro institutions.

Source: Opportunity costs were derived from regression equations. Tuition and fee costs were computed from data on 950 colleges and universities for 1960-61 in The Cost of Four Years of College (distributed by the New York Life Insurance Company).

cause their inclusion would not appreciably alter the results. Had this cost been included, the attractiveness of the investment in a college education characterized by higher opportunity and tuition and fee costs would have been slightly reduced relative to the investment involving lower outlays and opportunity costs.

The procedure of computing rates of return based on the same income stream for each of the groups by type of institution attended implicitly assumes that the abilities of the students, their socio-economic background, and the quality of education received were approximately equal, as between private and public colleges and universities. While this assumption is obviously suspect between individual institutions, it was felt that in terms of broad averages the assumption was not unrealistic. The differences in rates of return between the types of institution attended amounted to about 1.5 percentage points for students with no earnings for each group except South nonwhite males (Table 22). When the costs are combined for private and public colleges, the differences in rates of return to students with no earnings between regions and races are approximately the same as those indicated earlier (again see Table 19). These rates of return over the average of private and public college costs for four years were somewhat below the marginal rate of return for completing the 13th year of school, and somewhat above the rate for completing the 16th year.

Rates of return over costs were also computed assuming that 20 and 30 per cent of opportunity costs were earned while attending college; to estimate the impact which part-time employment would have on the attractiveness of the investment decision. Part-time earnings were based on the opportunity costs rather than all costs because it was felt that this would better allow for employment opportunities and earnings possibilities for the various racial and regional groups. The effects

TABLE 22

Internal Rates of Return on an Investment in a Four-Year College Education For Males by Region, Race, Type of Institution Attended, and Specified Percentage of Opportunity Costs Earned While Attending College.*

| | Rate of Return Assuming: | | | | | | | | |
| | Attendance at a Private College | | | Attendance at a Public College | | | Average of Public and Private College Costs | | |
Region and Race	No Earnings	20 Per Cent of Opportunity Costs Earned	30 Per Cent of Opportunity Costs Earned	No Earnings	20 Per Cent of Opportunity Costs Earned	30 Per Cent of Opportunity Costs Earned	No Earnings	20 Per Cent of Opportunity Costs Earned	30 Per Cent of Opportunity Costs Earned
Nonsouth White Males	10.0	11.0	11.5	11.5	13.0	14.0	10.5	12.0	13.0
Nonsouth Nonwhite Males	4.5	5.5	6.0	6.0	7.5	8.5	5.5	6.5	7.0
South White Males	11.5	13.0	14.0	13.0	15.0	16.0	12.0	14.5	15.5
South Nonwhite Males	7.0	8.0	9.0	7.5	9.0	10.0	7.5	8.5	9.5

* All rates of return rounded to the nearest half-percentage point.
Source: Computed from data presented in Tables 11 and 21.

44

of part-time employment while attending college appreciably increased the rates of return to a college education for all groups.[13] The effects were most pronounced for those attending public colleges and universities because of the relatively greater significance of opportunity costs as a component of total costs for these persons. The percentage-point gain in the rates of return of South nonwhites as a result of earnings while in college was less than for the rest of the categories. Receipt of scholarships for attending colleges would also increase the value of the college investment in similar fashion. Complete tuition and fee scholarships in private colleges would have a greater impact on the rates of return to persons attending these institutions than would these same type of awards in the public institutions.

Comparison of the rates of return to college education with and without part-time employment and earnings also may reveal the cost of leisure time while pursuing a college education. The reduction in rates of return may be thought of as the price paid for leisure time, assuming of course that the released time was so employed rather than applied to the educational effort.[14]

13. It is assumed that participation in part-time employment had no effect on income after completion of college.
14. I am indebted to Professor Mary Jean Bowman for this point.

4. SOME IMPLICATIONS

The relatively low variation in income "explained" by the regression of income on years of school completed, even though statistically significant, is indicative of the existence of unspecified variables which are important determinants of income. It is not the intent here to enumerate or analyze the effects of such variables as ability, determination, or socio-economic background. However, certain factors are closely related to the composition of the income and education data, and to the completeness of the education variable itself. To begin with, the composition of the distributions analyzed could hardly be considered homogeneous, even when stratified by race, sex, age, urban-rural residence, and region. If it were possible to stratify the data further by occupation and industry, the correlation between income and education would increase, at least for some segments of the population. Furthermore, expression of the education variable in terms of formal schooling alone omits the influence of on-the-job training, trade schools, and apprenticeship programs on income. These educational activities are significant, both in terms of costs and returns.[1] Finally, a significant element of education which is unaccounted for is that found in the home, where the amount of knowledge imparted is of considerable import, even when compared to that transmitted at school.[2]

The substantial increases in correlation between income and education which took place between 1949 and 1959 are indicative of the increasing importance of formal education as the economy becomes more complex. Such increases could

1. See Jacob Mincer, "On-the-Job Training: Costs, Returns, and Some Implications," *The Journal of Political Economy*, Supplement, October, 1962, pp. 50-73.
2. See Fritz Machlup, *The Production and Distribution of Knowledge in the United States*, Princeton, Princeton University Press, 1962, pp. 52-56.

also result from increased quality of education. Increases in the association of income and education are to be expected in the future, perhaps in even greater magnitudes.

The differences in correlation coefficients between the various race, sex, urban-rural, and regional classes suggest that the educational investment will be evaluated in different terms by class. The lower percentage of the variation in income "explained" by education for nonwhites, in particular, indicates higher private rates of discount for evaluating an investment decision whose outcome is subject to greater relative variation. On the other hand, the low correlation between income and education for white females is the result of lower full-time labor force participation, rather than the lack of association between income and education. If data were available for only those white females in the full-time labor force, the degree of association between income and education for the group would no doubt be increased appreciably.

The regression coefficients (additional income per additional year of school completed) were considerably influenced by age within the various groups, and were significantly different between most groupings. The gains to nonwhites, in particular, from an additional year of school were low, and the magnitude of the differences between whites and nonwhites was most pronounced in the middle age classes.

It was suggested quite early in this study that the regression coefficients were an imperfect measure of the additional income associated with additional schooling because of the known but unquantifiable differences in the quality of a year of school. If the quality of the years of school completed variable could be standardized in terms of that received by Nonsouth white males, the values of the regression coefficients of the other male groups would be increased, as would the number of calendar years and the costs required for mem-

47

bers of these groups to achieve the equivalent of this "standard" year. It is quite possible that increased quality of education for a given number of years of school for South nonwhites, particularly, might yield higher returns than just an increase in mean educational achievement in this group.

The use of the linear regression technique has the disadvantage of attaching equal monetary weight to each year of school completed. This of course constitutes one of the major weaknesses of the procedures employed. However, the regression coefficients for the earlier years of school completed do not overstate the economic significance of these years as much as might be expected. In essence, these early years are the foundation for further education and have an "option" value in that successful completion gives rise to the alternative of additional education and the additional income associated with it.[3] Furthermore, the correlation and regression analysis provides measures of the degree of association of income and education, which are highly useful in analyzing the differences among important segments of the population.

The private incentives to invest in education are highly variable between groups. Typically, the incomes of nonwhite males are below those of white males at given levels of education, and the disparity increases with the level of educational attainment. These differing incentives also exist when expressed in terms of rates of return to education over cost. However, it appears that incentives as measured by rates of return to invest in education by South males were higher than for their Nonsouth counterparts in both 1949 and 1959. While the phenomenon suggests that average educational achievement might be higher for South males than for their Nonsouth counterparts, there are several other factors which in-

---

3. For a discussion of this point see, B. A. Weisbrod, "Education and Investment in Human Capital," *The Journal of Political Economy*, Supplement, October, 1962, pp. 109-14.

fluence the education decision which may offset the higher incentives of South males. To begin with, Professor Nicholls has pointed out that the general southern attitude has been anti-education, which in and of itself would tend to reduce the average educational attainment in this area.[4] Furthermore, the family resources available to assist children in pursuing education have been lower in the South than in many other areas. In addition, there may be less awareness of the returns to education in a traditionally non-industrial region than in a more highly developed area. Finally, it might be suspected that the rates of return in the South would be lowered if the Bureau of the Census did not include the District of Columbia, Maryland, and Delaware in its definition of the South. For example, the regression coefficient for white males age 25 and over was $428 for six southeastern states as contrasted with $473 for white males in this age category in all of the "Southern states." Unfortunately, Census data for the individual states are not given by age, and thus investigation of the incentives to invest in education in the more traditionally defined South is precluded.

The differential incentives to invest in education among the various race, urban-rural, and regional classifications also have implications for enhancing the value of human capital through greater occupational and geographic mobility. While these differences may be in part reflective of the quality of education received by, or available to, the various classes, they are also indicative of limited geographic mobility, and differential access to, and treatment in, the various occupations. It is an obviously inefficient use of both private and public resources to invest in human capital through education when there are racial or sex limitations which prevent the human capital from being employed in its highest and best

4. W. H. Nicholls, "Southern Tradition and Regional Economic Progress," *The Southern Economic Journal*, January, 1960, pp. 192, 193.

use. It is conceivable that increasing geographic and occupational mobility might enhance the value of the total stock of human capital by more than that which could be achieved just by raising the overall level of educational achievement.

If it is society's policy to increase the educational achievement, and thus the economic opportunities and incomes of disadvantaged groups, one approach would be to equalize the rates of return to education. For example, the economic incentives for nonwhites to complete a college education could be equalized, in terms of rates of return, by subsidizing the education of nonwhites. Payment of a lump sum subsidy of $5,236 to Nonsouth nonwhite males and $4,150 to South nonwhite males on completion of college would equalize the rates of return with their white counterparts.[5]

Finally, while there are a host of non-economic factors which influence the education decision and many non-economic benefits are derived from education, there was no intent to disparage the importance of these factors and benefits by omitting them from the discussion here. On the other hand, the economic costs of, and returns to, education are of such significance in the educational decision that they must be given prominence in evaluating society's educational policies and programs.

5. The amounts of these subsidies were determined by obtaining the present values of the lifetime incomes of nonwhites at the rates of return to whites over the average of costs in private and public colleges. The subsidies would be the differences between their present values and the costs of college education for nonwhites. For the respective rates of return, again see Table 22.

SELECT BIBLIOGRAPHY

BOOKS AND MONOGRAPHS

BECKER, GARY S. *Human Capital.* New York: Columbia University Press, 1964.

BOWEN, W. G. *Economic Aspects of Education: Three Essays.* ("Research Report No. 104.") Princeton: Industrial Relations Section, Department of Economics, Princeton University, 1964.

MACHLUP, FRITZ. *The Production and Distribution of Knowledge in the United States.* Princeton: Princeton University Press, 1962.

MILLER, HERMAN P. *Income of the American People.* New York: John Wiley & Sons, 1955.

MUSHKIN, SELMA J. (ed.). *Economics of Higher Education.* (OE-50027, Bulletin, 1962, No. 5.) Washington: U.S. Government Printing Office, 1962.

SCHULTZ, T. W. *The Economic Value of Education.* New York: Columbia University Press, 1963.

VAIZEY, JOHN. *The Economics of Education.* Glencoe, Ill.: Free Press, 1962.

WEISBROD, B. A. *External Benefits of Public Education: An Economic Appraisal.* ("Research Report No. 105.") Princeton: Industrial Relations Section, Department of Economics, Princeton University, 1964.

51

INCOME AND EDUCATIONAL ACHIEVEMENT

ARTICLES

BECKER, GARY S. "Underinvestment in College Education?" *American Economic Review*, May, 1960, pp. 346-54.

————. "Investment in Human Capital: A Theoretical Analysis," *The Journal of Political Economy*, Supplement, October, 1962, pp. 9-49.

DENISON, EDWARD F. "Education, Economic Growth, and Gaps in Information," *The Journal of Political Economy*, Supplement, October, 1962, pp. 124-28.

HANSEN, W. LEE. "Total and Private Rates of Return to Investment in Schooling," *The Journal of Political Economy*, April, 1963, pp. 128-40.

HOUTHAKKER, H. S. "Education and Income," *Review of Economics and Statistics*, February, 1959, pp. 24-28.

LASSITER, ROY L., JR. "The Association of Income and Education for Males by Region, Race, and Age," *The Southern Economic Journal*, July, 1965, pp. 15-22.

MILLER, HERMAN P. "Annual and Lifetime Income in Relation to Education, 1939-1959," *American Economic Review*, December, 1960, pp. 962-86.

MINCER, JACOB. "Investment in Human Capital and Personal Income Distribution," *The Journal of Political Economy*, August, 1958, pp. 281-302.

————. "On-the-Job Training: Costs, Returns, and Some Implications," *The Journal of Political Economy*, Supplement, October, 1962, pp. 50-79.

SCHULTZ, THEODORE W. "Capital Formation by Education," *The Journal of Political Economy*, December, 1960, pp. 571-83.

————. "Investment in Human Capital," *American Economic Review*, March, 1961, pp. 1-17.

————. "Reflections on Investment in Man," *The Journal of Political Economy*, Supplement, October, 1962, pp. 1-8.

WEISBROD, BURTON A. "The Valuation of Human Capital," *The Journal of Political Economy*, October, 1961, pp. 425-36.

————. "Education and Investment in Human Capital," *The Journal of Political Economy*, Supplement, October, 1962, pp. 106-23.

UNIVERSITY OF FLORIDA MONOGRAPHS

Social Sciences

1. *The Whigs of Florida, 1845-1854,* by H. J. Doherty, Jr.

2. *Austrian Catholics and the Social Question, 1918-1933,* by A. Diamant.

3. *The Siege of St. Augustine in 1702,* by C. W. Arnade

4. *New Light on Early and Medieval Japanese Historiography,* by J. A. Harrison

5. *The Swiss Press and Foreign Affairs in World War II,* by F. H. Hartmann

6. *The American Militia: Decade of Decision 1789-1800,* by J. K. Mahon

7. *The Foundation of Jacques Maritain's Political Philosophy,* by H. Y. Jung

8. *Latin American Population Studies,* by T. L. Smith

9. *Jacksonian Democracy on the Florida Frontier,* by A. W. Thompson

10. *Holman Versus Hughes: Extension of Australian Commonwealth Powers,* by C. Joyner

11. *Welfare Economics and Subsidy Programs,* by M. Z. Kafoglis

12. *Tribune of the Slavophiles: Konstantin Aksakov,* by Edw. Chmielewski

13. *City Managers in Politics: An Analysis of Manager Tenure and Termination,* by G. M. Kammerer, C. D. Farris, J. M. DeGrove, and A. B. Clubok.

14. *Recent Southern Economic Development as Revealed by the Changing Structure of Employment,* by E. S. Dunn, Jr.

15. *Sea Power and Chilean Independence,* by D. E. Worcester

16. *The Sherman Antitrust Act and Foreign Trade,* by A. Simmons

17. *The Origins of Hamilton's Fiscal Policies,* by D. F. Swanson

18. *Criminal Asylum in Anglo-Saxon Law,* by C. H. Riggs, Jr.

19. *Colonia Barón Hirsch, A Jewish Agricultural Colony in Argentina,* by M. D. Winsberg

20. *Time Deposits in Present-day Commercial Banking,* by L. L. Crum

21. *The Eastern Greenland Case in Historical Perspective,* by O. Svarlien

22. *Jacksonian Democracy and the Historians,* by A. A. Cave

23. *The Rise of the American Chemistry Profession, 1850-1900,* by E. H. Beardsley

24. *Aymara Communities and the Bolivian Agrarian Reform,* by W. E. Carter

25. *Conservatives in the Progressive Era: The Taft Republicans of 1912,* by N. M. Wilensky

26. *The Anglo-Norwegian Fisheries Case of 1951 and the Changing Law of the Territorial Sea,* by T. Kobayashi

27. *The Liquidity Structure of Firms and Monetary Economics,* by W. J. Frazer, Jr.

28. *Russo-Persian Commercial Relations, 1828-1914,* by M. L. Entner

29. *The Imperial Policy of Sir Robert Borden,* by H. A. Wilson

30. *The Association of Income and Educational Achievement,* by R. L. Lassiter, Jr.